“ECHOES OF THE HIMALAYAS: TALES FROM KASHMIR”

“A DEEP DIVE INTO THE UNIQUE CULTURE AND HISTORY OF KASHMIR”

ZUHAAN MANZOOR

Copyright © Zuhaan Manzoor
All Rights Reserved.

This book has been self-published with all reasonable efforts taken to make the material error-free by the author. No part of this book shall be used, reproduced in any manner whatsoever without written permission from the author, except in the case of brief quotations embodied in critical articles and reviews.

The Author of this book is solely responsible and liable for its content including but not limited to the views, representations, descriptions, statements, information, opinions and references ["Content"]. The Content of this book shall not constitute or be construed or deemed to reflect the opinion or expression of the Publisher or Editor. Neither the Publisher nor Editor endorse or approve the Content of this book or guarantee the reliability, accuracy or completeness of the Content published herein and do not make any representations or warranties of any kind, express or implied, including but not limited to the implied warranties of merchantability, fitness for a particular purpose. The Publisher and Editor shall not be liable whatsoever for any errors, omissions, whether such errors or omissions result from negligence, accident, or any other cause or claims for loss or damages of any kind, including without limitation, indirect or consequential loss or damage arising out of use, inability to use, or about the reliability, accuracy or sufficiency of the information contained in this book.

Made with ♥ on the Notion Press Platform
www.notionpress.com

"Echoes of the Himalayas: Tales from Kashmir":

Dedicated to the people of Kashmir, whose stories and traditions have enriched our world with their beauty and depth. May this book honor your rich cultural heritage and inspire future generations to learn more about your enduring legacy. Special thanks to the authors, editors, and researchers whose hard work and dedication brought these tales to life, and to all those who supported the creation of this book. May its pages resonate with readers far and wide, carrying the echoes of the Himalayas across time and space.

To the people of Kashmir, who have faced countless challenges throughout their history with resilience and grace. This book is dedicated to you, in recognition of your rich cultural heritage and the countless stories and traditions that you have shared with the world. Your art, music, literature, and poetry are a testament to your enduring spirit and the beauty of your homeland.

To the authors, editors, and researchers who worked tirelessly to bring these stories to life, thank you for your dedication and hard work. Your efforts have helped to preserve and share the stories and traditions of Kashmir with a wider audience, and for that, we are grateful.

To all those who supported the creation of this book, we extend our deepest appreciation. Your contributions helped to ensure that these tales of the Himalayas would be heard and that the culture of Kashmir would be celebrated and honored.

May this book serve as a tribute to the people of Kashmir and their incredible spirit, and as an inspiration to others to learn more about this remarkable region and its people. May it help to foster a greater understanding and appreciation of the power of storytelling to connect us all, across time and space.

Contents

Contents

Foreword

The Himalayas are home to some of the most majestic and awe-inspiring landscapes on earth. But beyond the beauty of the mountains lies a world of stories, traditions, and culture that is just as rich and enchanting. In this book, "Echoes of the Himalayas: Tales from Kashmir," we have the privilege of exploring the many facets of this fascinating region through the lens of its stories and folktales.

Kashmir, in particular, has a long and storied history, with a rich and vibrant culture that has endured for centuries. From its art and architecture to its music and poetry, Kashmir has inspired countless generations with its beauty and grace. In this book, we have the opportunity to explore some of the many tales and legends that have emerged from this incredible region, each one a window into the soul of Kashmir.

Through the stories in this book, we meet heroes and villains, and a host of other characters who embody the spirit and character of the Himalayan people. From the epic battles between good and evil to the gentle wisdom of everyday life, each tale offers a unique perspective on the challenges and triumphs of the human experience.

This book is the result of years of research, and the contributions of many dedicated individuals who have worked tirelessly to bring these stories to light. We hope that it will serve as a tribute to the people of Kashmir and the Himalayas, and an inspiration to readers around the world to learn more about this remarkable region and its many treasures.

As you embark on this journey through the stories of the Himalayas, we invite you to let your imagination soar and your heart be filled with wonder. The tales in this book are like echoes, ringing out across the ages and reminding us of the power of storytelling to connect us all, across time and space. Enjoy the journey!

Preface

The Himalayas have long been a source of wonder and inspiration for people around the world. The rugged peaks, snow-capped mountains, and pristine valleys are among the most spectacular natural wonders on earth. But beyond the breathtaking scenery lies a world of stories, traditions, and culture that is just as rich and enchanting.

Kashmir, in particular, has a long and fascinating history, with a cultural heritage that spans thousands of years. The region has been the site of epic battles, legendary romances, and a wealth of art, music, and literature. In this book, "Echoes of the Himalayas: Tales from Kashmir," we have the privilege of exploring some of the many stories and folktales that have emerged from this remarkable region.

Our goal in compiling this book was to create a comprehensive collection of stories that would offer readers a glimpse into the heart and soul of Kashmir. We wanted to capture the essence of the region's cultural heritage, from its myths and legends to its everyday wisdom and humor. We also wanted to create a work that would be accessible to a wide range of readers, from those who are just discovering the magic of the Himalayas to those who are already deeply immersed in the region's culture and traditions.

To that end, we have assembled a diverse collection of tales, each one offering a unique perspective on the region and its people. Some of the stories are ancient, handed down from generation to generation through oral tradition. Others are more recent, reflecting the changing face of Kashmir in the modern era. But all of the stories in this book share one thing in common: they are a testament to the enduring spirit of the Himalayan people and the richness of their cultural heritage.

We would like to express our sincere gratitude to the countless individuals who contributed to the creation of this book. We are deeply indebted to the storytellers and folklorists who shared their knowledge and expertise with us, and to the editors, artists, and designers who helped to bring these stories to life. We are also grateful to the people of Kashmir and the Himalayas, whose culture and traditions have inspired us and countless others around the world.

As you read the stories in this book, we invite you to take a journey through the ages and experience the magic of the Himalayas for yourself.

We hope that these tales will inspire you, delight you, and enrich your understanding of this remarkable region and its people. Enjoy the journey!

Acknowledgements

Creating this book has been a labor of love, and it would not have been possible without the contributions and support of many individuals and organizations. We would like to take this opportunity to express our deepest gratitude to all those who have helped us along the way.

First and foremost, we would like to thank the people of Kashmir and the Himalayas, whose culture and traditions have been the source of inspiration for this book. We are deeply grateful for the generosity and hospitality that we have received from the communities we have visited, and for the warmth and kindness of the people we have met.

We would also like to thank the many storytellers and folklorists who shared their knowledge and expertise with us. Their passion and dedication to preserving the rich cultural heritage of the Kashmir has been a constant source of inspiration, and we are grateful for the opportunity to learn from them.

We are also indebted to the many individuals and organizations who supported us during the research and writing of this book. We would like to thank the editors, artists, and designers who helped to bring these stories to life, and the publishers who believed in our vision and supported our efforts.

Last but not least, we would like to express our deepest gratitude to our families and friends, who provided us with unwavering support and encouragement throughout the process of creating this book. Their love and encouragement have been a constant source of inspiration and motivation, and we are forever grateful for their presence in our lives.

In short, this book is the result of the collective effort and dedication of many individuals, and we are grateful to all those who have contributed to its creation. We hope that it will serve as a tribute to the people of Kashmir and the Himalayas, and an inspiration to readers around the world to learn more about this remarkable region and its many treasures.

Prologue

The Himalayas are a place of myth and mystery, a land where the gods are said to reside and the very earth seems to speak. For thousands of years, people have been drawn to this rugged, beautiful region, captivated by its breathtaking scenery and rich cultural heritage.

Among the many treasures of the Himalayas, few are more enchanting than the stories and folktales that have emerged from this remarkable region. These tales are a testament to the enduring spirit of the Himalayan people, and the depth and richness of their cultural traditions.

In this book, "Echoes of the Himalayas: Tales from Kashmir," we have the privilege of exploring some of the many stories and legends that have emerged from one of the most fascinating regions of the Himalayas: Kashmir. Nestled in the heart of the Himalayan mountain range, Kashmir has long been regarded as one of the most beautiful and spiritually significant places on earth. Its stunning natural beauty and rich cultural heritage have inspired countless writers, artists, and travelers throughout history.

The stories in this book are drawn from a variety of sources, ranging from ancient oral traditions to contemporary literature. Some are cautionary tales, warning of the dangers of greed, pride, and jealousy. Others are tales of love and romance, celebrating the enduring bonds of family and community. Still others are tales of heroism and adventure, capturing the courage and resourcefulness of the people of Kashmir in the face of danger and adversity.

Throughout these tales, we glimpse the soul of a people who have endured countless trials and tribulations throughout history, but who have emerged stronger and more resilient than ever. We witness their enduring faith in the power of community, the importance of tradition, and the unbreakable bonds of family and friendship.

In the pages that follow, we invite you to journey with us into the heart of the Himalayas and discover the magic of Kashmir for yourself. Through the tales that we share, we hope to offer a glimpse into the rich cultural heritage of this remarkable region, and to inspire readers around the world to learn more about the many treasures of the Himalayas. Enjoy the journey!

CHAPTER ONE

“The Legend of the Valley”: An introduction to the rich history and culture of Kashmir, and the enduring myths and legends that have shaped the region

KASHMIR

The Kashmir Valley has always been shrouded in mystery and legend. The stunning natural beauty of this Himalayan region has long been a draw for travelers, and the region's rich culture and history only add to its allure. According to local lore, the valley was once a great lake, until a saint named Kashyap drained it with a stroke of his staff, revealing the lush green valley we know today.

Despite its idyllic setting, however, Kashmir has often been a site of conflict and turmoil. For centuries, the region was ruled by a succession of powerful dynasties, including the Mughals and the Sikhs. In the mid-19th century, the British East India Company gained control of Kashmir, setting the stage for a long and bloody struggle for independence.

Today, the region remains a disputed territory, with both India and Pakistan claiming it as their own. Despite the ongoing political and military tensions, however, the people of Kashmir have a deep and abiding love for their land and its many wonders.

One of the most famous legends associated with the valley is the tale of the sage Kashyap. According to local lore, Kashyap was troubled by the lake that covered the valley, as it was home to a demon who terrorized the local people. In a fit of anger, Kashyap struck the lake with his staff, causing the waters to recede and revealing the fertile land below. The demon was vanquished, and the grateful people of the valley named their home after the sage who had saved them.

Another popular legend tells of a princess who fell in love with a young man from a rival kingdom. The two were unable to marry due to the longstanding enmity between their families, so they made a secret pact to meet in a secret grove of chinar trees every night. Over time, the grove became a place of great power and beauty, and it was said that those who visited it would find their deepest desires fulfilled. Eventually, the two lovers were discovered and killed, but their legend lived on, and the chinar grove remains a place of great significance to this day.

Despite the many legends and stories associated with the valley, however, the people of Kashmir are all too aware of the dark side of their history. In recent decades, the region has been wracked by violence and conflict, as separatist movements have clashed with the Indian military. Thousands of people have been killed or displaced, and the ongoing tensions have left many feeling uncertain and afraid.

Despite this, however, the people of Kashmir remain deeply connected to their land and their culture. Whether through music, poetry, or elaborate festivals that take place throughout the year, the people of Kashmir are determined to preserve their heritage and their identity, even in the face of overwhelming challenges.

As the sun sets over the Himalayas, the valley of Kashmir glows with a quiet, unyielding beauty. The mountains loom large in the distance, their jagged peaks softened by the purple haze of twilight. In the villages and towns that dot the valley, families gather for evening meals, telling stories and sharing laughter in the warm glow of lanterns and fires.

Despite the many challenges that the people of Kashmir face, their spirit remains unbroken. For them, the valley is more than just a physical place; it is a home, a refuge, and a source of deep and abiding pride. It is a place of legends and stories, but also of courage and resilience, and it will continue to inspire and captivate all who are fortunate enough to experience its magic.

In addition to its natural beauty and rich culture, the Kashmir Valley has long been known for its stunning architecture, particularly its impressive mosques, and shrines. One of the most famous of these is the Hazratbal Shrine, which is said to house the sacred hair of the Prophet Muhammad. The shrine is a popular pilgrimage site for Muslims from around the world, and its white marble exterior and towering minarets make it a breathtaking sight.

Another notable feature of the valley is its unique cuisine, which blends flavors from the Indian subcontinent, Central Asia, and the Middle East. Some of the most popular dishes include rogan josh, a rich lamb curry, and wazwan, a multi-course meal that is traditionally served at weddings and other special occasions. The valley is also known for its tea culture, with countless tea houses serving up piping hot cups of kahwa, a fragrant tea made with saffron, almonds, and cinnamon.

Despite the many challenges facing the people of Kashmir, the valley remains a place of great beauty and wonder, and its legends and stories continue to captivate the imagination of all who hear them. As the sun rises over the snow-capped peaks of the Himalayas, the valley comes to life once again, and its people, with their deep and abiding love for their home, are determined to carry on and preserve its legacy for generations to come.

CHAPTER TWO

"A River Runs Through It": A journey along the Jhelum River, exploring the many towns and villages that line its banks, and the people who call them

The Jhelum River is one of the most important waterways in the Kashmir Valley. It originates in the Himalayas and flows through the heart of the valley, eventually empty

DAL LAKE

ing into the Chenab River. Along the way, it passes through dozens of towns and villages, each with its own unique character and charm.

As we set out on our journey along the Jhelum, we are immediately struck by the stunning natural beauty that surrounds us. The snow-capped peaks of the Himalayas looming in the distance, while the lush green banks of the river are dotted with wildflowers and towering trees.

Our first stop is the town of Baramulla, which sits on the northern bank of the Jhelum. Baramulla is one of the oldest towns in the valley, and it has a rich history that dates back to the 6th century. We stroll through the narrow streets, taking in the colorful storefronts and bustling marketplaces. We stop at a tea shop and sample a cup of kahwa, a local tea made with saffron and spices.

As we continue along the river, we come to the town of Sopore. This is an important agricultural center in the valley, known for its apple orchards and saffron fields. We meet a local farmer who shows us his fields and explains the process of harvesting saffron. It is a labor-intensive process, but the rewards are great, as saffron is one of the most valuable spices in the world.

Our next stop is the town of Shalimar, which is famous for its gardens. The Shalimar Bagh is a stunning Mughal-era garden that is a UNESCO World Heritage Site. We wander through the terraced gardens, taking in the fragrant flowers and intricate water features. We pause by a tranquil pool, where a group of young musicians are playing traditional Kashmiri music on the santoor and tabla.

As we move further down the river, we come to the town of Srinagar, which is the largest city in the valley. Srinagar is a bustling metropolis, with a rich history that dates back to the 3rd century BC. We explore the winding alleys of the Old City, taking in the ancient mosques and historic homes. We stop at a spice market and marvel at the colorful piles of cumin, turmeric, and ginger.

As we continue our journey, we come to the town of Anantnag, which is an important center of Islamic scholarship in the valley. We visit a madrasa, or religious school, where young students are studying the Quran and learning the principles of Islamic law. We speak with the headmaster, who tells us about the school's long history and its commitment to promoting education and tolerance.

Our final stop is the town of Shopian, which is known for its stunning apple orchards. We meet a local farmer who takes us on a tour of his orchard, pointing out the different varieties of apples and explaining the process of cultivation. He tells us about the challenges of farming in the valley, including unpredictable weather patterns and the ongoing political tensions.

As our journey along the Jhelum comes to an end, we are struck by the incredible diversity and resilience of the people who call this river home. Despite the many challenges they face, from political instability to environmental degradation, they remain deeply connected to their land and their culture. They are committed to preserving their heritage and their way of life, and they are determined to pass it on to future generations.

As we gaze out over the shimmering waters of the Jhelum, we are filled with a sense of wonder and awe. This river has been a source of life and inspiration for centuries, and it will continue to be so for generations to come.

CHAPTER THREE

"The Houseboat on Dal Lake": A closer look at the unique houseboats that dot Srinagar's famous Dal Lake, and the fascinating stories of the families

HOUSE BOAT

The houseboats of Dal Lake are some of the most iconic symbols of Kashmiri culture. These floating homes are a unique blend of traditional craftsmanship and modern luxury, providing an unforgettable experience for visitors to the valley. But beyond their ornate wood carvings and opulent interiors, these houseboats are also the homes of families who have lived on them for generations, and who have fascinating stories to tell about their way of life.

As we board one of the houseboats, we are immediately struck by the intricate woodwork and the sumptuous fabrics that adorn the interior. Our host, Zuhaan, welcomes us warmly and offers us a cup of kahwa, the traditional Kashmiri tea made with saffron and spices. As we sip our tea, Zuhaan begins to tell us about the history of the houseboats on Dal Lake.

"Many years ago, when the British ruled India, they came to Kashmir to escape the heat of the plains. They built grand houses and hotels along the shores of Dal Lake, but the Maharaja of Kashmir decreed that no new buildings could be constructed on the lake itself. So the British came up with a clever solution - they built houseboats. And so began the tradition of the houseboats on Dal Lake."

As we listen to Zuhaan's story, we realize that these houseboats are not just a tourist attraction, but a living legacy of Kashmiri history and culture. Zuhaan tells us that his family has been living on this houseboat for three generations, and that he himself was born and raised here. He shows us photographs of his parents and grandparents, and tells us stories about their lives on the boat.

"Life on the houseboat is not always easy," he says. "We have to rely on generators for electricity, and sometimes the lake freezes over in the winter, making it difficult to get supplies. But we love our way of life, and we wouldn't trade it for anything."

As we explore the houseboat, we are struck by the attention to detail and the sense of history that permeates every corner. The walls are adorned with antique maps and photographs of old Srinagar, while the furniture is a blend of traditional Kashmiri designs and modern comforts. Zuhaan tells us that the wood used to build the houseboat is deodar, a type of cedar tree that is native to the Himalayas.

"We use only the finest materials," he says. "Every piece of wood is carefully selected and carved by hand. And the carpets and fabrics are woven by local artisans, using techniques that have been passed down through the generations."

As we settle in for the night, we are lulled to sleep by the gentle rocking of the houseboat and the sound of the water lapping against the hull. The next morning, we wake up to a stunning view of the lake, with its misty mornings and shimmering waters. We take a shikara, or traditional wooden boat, across the lake to explore some of the other houseboats.

We meet a family who has been living on their houseboat for over four generations. The patriarch, Abdul, tells us about the changes he has seen in his lifetime.

"When I was young, there were only a few dozen houseboats on the lake. Now there are hundreds. And tourism has changed our way of life in many ways. But we are proud of our culture, and we are determined to preserve it for future generations."

Abdul tells us about the Kashmiri art and handicrafts that have been passed down through his family, including wood carving, embroidery, and paper mache. He shows us some of the beautiful pieces his family has created, including intricate jewelry boxes and ornate picture frames.

As we continue our journey, we meet other families who have fascinating stories to tell. We hear

about the challenges and joys of living on a houseboat, from the difficulties of maintaining the boats in a harsh climate to the sense of community and family that is fostered by living in such close quarters.

One family we meet, the Mirs, are well-known for their hospitality and their delicious traditional Kashmiri meals. As we sit down to dinner on their houseboat, we are treated to a feast of rogan josh, a rich lamb curry, and saffron rice, accompanied by tangy chutneys and freshly baked naan bread.

"Our food is our way of sharing our culture with others," says Mrs. Mir. "We want to show people the real Kashmir, not just the tourist attractions."

As we savor the flavors of the meal, we realize that the houseboats of Dal Lake are not just a place to stay, but a window into a unique way of life that is intimately tied to the culture and history of Kashmir.

As our journey comes to an end, we reflect on the many stories we have heard and the people we have met along the way. The houseboats of Dal Lake are not just floating hotels, but a testament to the resilience and creativity of the Kashmiri people.

As we say goodbye to our hosts and make our way back to the shore, we realize that we have been privileged to be a part of this vibrant and welcoming community, if only for a short while. The memories of the houseboats on Dal Lake will stay with us forever, and we are grateful for the opportunity to have experienced this unique and beautiful way of life.

CHAPTER FOUR

"The Floating Gardens of Nishat Bagh": A visit to one of Kashmir's most beautiful Mughal gardens, and the story of the incredible feats of engineering

NISHAT GARDEN

We arrive at Nishat Bagh, a beautiful Mughal garden that sits on the eastern shore of Dal Lake. As we enter the gates, we are struck by the lush greenery that surrounds us. The garden is a paradise of terraced lawns, cascading fountains, and flowering trees.

Our guide, local author Zuhaan Manzoor, explains that the garden was built by the Mughal Emperor Jahangir in the early 17th century. He wanted to create a beautiful retreat for himself and his wife, Nur Jahan, and to showcase the wealth and power of his empire.

But what makes Nishat Bagh truly remarkable are the "floating gardens" - beds of soil and vegetation that are suspended on a bed of water, creating the illusion that they are floating on the surface of the lake.

Zuhaan tells us the incredible story of how these gardens were created. It required an incredible feat of engineering and planning, with workers digging deep channels in the lake bed and creating a network of canals and sluices to control the flow of water.

The soil for the gardens had to be brought in by boat, and carefully arranged in layers to create a stable foundation for the plants. The gardeners had to be skilled at selecting the right plants and managing the delicate balance of soil, water, and nutrients.

As we walk through the gardens, we are struck by the ingenuity and dedication of the people who created them. We see locals tending to the gardens, carefully pruning and watering the plants.

Zuhaan explains that the floating gardens are not just beautiful, but also serve an important purpose in the community. They provide a source of food and income for the local people, who cultivate vegetables and flowers that are sold at markets in Srinagar.

We stop to talk to a group of gardeners, who tell us about the challenges of living and working on the lake. They face constant threats from rising water levels, pollution, and changing weather patterns, but they are committed to preserving the beauty and heritage of Nishat Bagh for future generations.

As we leave the garden, we are struck by the incredible spirit of resilience and creativity that we have encountered in Kashmir. The floating gardens of Nishat Bagh are not just a testament to the ingenuity of the Mughal engineers, but also to the resourcefulness and determination of the people who continue to maintain them.

We are grateful for the opportunity to have experienced this unique and beautiful corner of the world, and to have met the amazing people who call it home. The memories of the floating gardens of Nishat Bagh will stay with us forever, a testament to the enduring beauty and resilience of the human spirit.As we continue our walk through the gardens, Zuhaan points out some of the different plants and flowers that are grown here. We see patches of colorful marigolds, fragrant roses, and rows of vegetables like spinach and turnips.

The floating gardens are not just a unique feature of Nishat Bagh, but also an important part of the local economy. The vegetables and flowers grown here are sold at markets in Srinagar, providing a source of income for the gardeners and their families.

We stop to talk to some of the gardeners, who are friendly and eager to share their stories with us. They tell us about the challenges of living and working on the lake, from dealing with unpredictable weather patterns to the constant threat of rising water levels.

Despite these challenges, they are committed to preserving the beauty and heritage of the gardens. They take great pride in their work, and it shows in the careful attention they pay to the plants and the water channels that sustain them.

As we make our way back to the shore, Zuhaan tells us more about the history of Nishat Bagh and its role in Kashmiri culture. He explains that the Mughal emperors were great patrons of the arts, and the gardens were not just a place for relaxation, but also a showcase for their wealth and power.

Over the centuries, the gardens have been visited by artists, poets, and travelers from all over the world, drawn to the beauty and serenity of the surroundings. Today, they continue to inspire and enchant visitors with their intricate designs and stunning natural beauty.

As we board our boat and make our way back across the lake, we are struck by the contrast between the chaos and noise of the city and the peaceful tranquility of the gardens. It's a reminder that even in the midst of turmoil and conflict, there are places of beauty and serenity that endure.

The floating gardens of Nishat Bagh are a testament to the resilience and creativity of the people of Kashmir, who have found ways to survive and thrive in the face of adversity. They are a symbol of the enduring beauty and power of nature, and the capacity of the human spirit to overcome even the greatest challenges. We feel grateful for the opportunity to have experienced them, and to have met the amazing people who call them home.

CHAPTER FIVE

“The Saffron Fields of Pampore”: An Exploration of the Delicate and Labor-Intensive Process of Cultivating Saffron, and the Many Traditions and Ritual

SAFFRON FEILDS

As we drive towards Pampore, the air is filled with the sweet aroma of saffron. Zuhaan tells us that this small town is known as the "saffron capital" of India and that the precious spice has been cultivated here for centuries.

As we arrive at the saffron fields, we are struck by the sea of purple flowers that stretch out before us. The delicate flowers, known as crocus sativus, are the source of the precious spice that is used in cuisines all over the world.

Zuhaan introduces us to some of the farmers who tend to the saffron fields, and they explain the labor-intensive process of cultivating the spice. Each flower must be carefully hand-picked, and the delicate red stigmas removed and dried.

It takes more than 75,000 flowers to produce just one pound of saffron, making it one of the most valuable spices in the world. The farmers take great pride in their work, and each step of the process is steeped in tradition and ritual.

We watch as the farmers carefully pluck the flowers and sort them into baskets. They then sit in a circle, carefully removing the delicate stigmas and laying them out on trays to dry in the sun.

As we walk through the fields, Zuhaan points out some of the different varieties of saffron and explains their unique flavor and aroma profiles. He tells us about the long history of saffron in Kashmiri culture and its many uses in traditional medicine and cuisine.

We stop to talk to some of the farmers, who are friendly and eager to share their stories with us. They tell us about the challenges of living and working in a region that has been plagued by conflict and political turmoil for decades.

Despite these challenges, they remain committed to their craft and to preserving the traditions and heritage of their ancestors. They take great pride in their work, and it shows in the care and attention they pay to each delicate flower.

As the sun begins to set, we make our way back to the car, feeling grateful for the opportunity to have experienced the magic of the saffron fields. We realize that the value of saffron extends far beyond its monetary worth; it is a symbol of the resilience and creativity of the people of Kashmir, and their deep connection to the land and the traditions that sustain them.

As we drive back to Srinagar, we reflect on the many stories we have heard and the many people we have met during our time in Kashmir. It is a land of great beauty and great complexity, of incredible warmth and hospitality, and of profound challenges and struggles.

We feel grateful to have been welcomed into this amazing community and to have had the opportunity to learn from Zuhaan and the many others who have shared their stories and their lives with us. We know that we will carry these experiences with us always and that they will continue to inspire us long after we have left this magical land of saffron, houseboats, and floating gardens.

CHAPTER SIX

"A Taste of Kashmir" A Tour of the Region's Most Famous Culinary Delights, from Rich Meat Dishes like Rogan Josh to Sweet Treats like Phirni and Kulfi

As I make my way through the crowded streets of Srinagar, the scent of spices and grilled meat fills my senses. Kashmiri cuisine is as rich an

WAZWAAN

d diverse as the region's history, with influences from Central Asia, Persia, and the Indian subcontinent. In this chapter, I will take you on a tour of some of the most famous and delicious dishes that Kashmir has to offer.

But before we dive into the culinary delights of the region, it's important to understand the cultural and historical context in which they developed. Kashmir has a long and complex history, with influences from various cultures and civilizations. The region was an important hub of the Silk Road trade route, connecting Central Asia with the Indian subcontinent. Over time, this led to a fusion of culinary traditions, resulting in the unique flavors and dishes that we know today.

One of the most iconic dishes of Kashmir is rogan josh, a rich and spicy lamb curry that is flavored with a blend of aromatic spices such as cardamom, cumin, and fennel. The dish is said to have originated in Persia and was brought to Kashmir by the Mughal emperors. Today, it is a staple of Kashmiri cuisine, and every family has its own version of the recipe.

I make my way to a small family-owned restaurant in the heart of Srinagar to sample their version of rogan josh. The meat is tender and succulent, falling off the bone, and the sauce is thick and velvety, with a subtle heat that lingers on the tongue. The dish is typically served with fluffy naan bread or steamed rice, and a side of tangy yogurt raita to cool the palate.

As I savor the flavors of the dish, I'm struck by how the spices and ingredients come together to create a symphony of taste and texture. This is the beauty of Kashmiri cuisine - it's not just about the individual ingredients, but the way in which they are combined and cooked that makes the dishes truly special.

Another popular dish in Kashmir is the kebab, a skewered and grilled meat dish that is typically made with lamb or chicken. The kebabs are marinated in a blend of spices and yogurt before being grilled over an open flame, resulting in tender and juicy meat with a charred and smoky flavor.

I visit a street food vendor who specializes in kebabs, and watch as he expertly skewers the meat and grills it to perfection. The smell of the sizzling meat is irresistible, and I can't wait to taste the finished product. As I take my first bite, I'm struck by how the spices and yogurt marinade have infused the meat, resulting in a burst of flavor with every bite.

No tour of Kashmiri cuisine would be complete without a taste of the region's famous desserts. Phirni, a creamy rice pudding flavored with saffron and cardamom, is a popular dessert that is typically served at special occasions such as weddings and festivals. The dish is simple yet decadent, with a rich and velvety texture that is balanced by the delicate flavor of the saffron.

I visit a family-owned sweet shop that has been making phirni for generations. The dish is served in small earthenware pots and is topped with slivers of almonds and pistachios. As I take my first spoonful, I'm transported to another world - the creamy texture and subtle flavors are a perfect end to a meal.

Another popular dessert in Kashmir is kulfi, a rich and creamy ice cream that is flavored with cardamom, pistachios, and rose water. The ice cream is traditionally made by slow-cooking milk until it has thickened and reduced, resulting in adiverse range of influences, the food in Kashmir is a reflection of its unique history and geography. Its location on the ancient Silk Road brought traders from all over Asia, and with them came new ingredients and cooking techniques. Over time, local cooks adapted these flavors and methods to suit their own tastes and local produce, resulting in a cuisine that is truly one-of-a-kind.

While many of the traditional dishes of Kashmir are meat-based, there is also plenty of vegetarian and even vegan options. One popular vegetarian dish is nadru yakhni, which features lotus roots cooked in a yogurt-based gravy. For those with a sweet tooth, phirni and kulfi are must-try desserts.

Despite the challenges faced by the region, including political unrest and natural disasters, the people of Kashmir continue to hold on to their rich culinary traditions. By taking a food tour of the region, travelers can not only experience the unique flavors of Kashmir, but also support the local economy and celebrate the resilience of its people.

CHAPTER SEVEN

"The Mountains of Ladakh": A journey to the northern reaches of Kashmir, where the stark beauty of the Ladakh region

LADAKH MOUNTAINS

As I stood atop the Khardung La pass, at a height of over 18,000 feet, the thin air made it difficult to catch my breath. Yet, the stunning vista of the surrounding mountains made me forget about the physical strain. The crisp air, the pristine landscape, and the sheer magnificence of the Ladakh region were overwhelming.

Located in the northernmost reaches of Kashmir, Ladakh is a

land of contrasts. The stark beauty of its mountainous terrain is juxtaposed with the vibrant culture of its people. A journey to this region is a journey into the heart of the Himalayas, and an exploration of its unique blend of nature and culture.

As I set out on my journey, I was struck by the remoteness of Ladakh. It is a region that has remained relatively untouched by the outside world, and this is evident in the simplicity of its people and their way of life. The Ladakhis are a proud and hardy people, whose lives are intrinsically linked to the land. They have developed a deep understanding and respect for their surroundings, and this is reflected in their way of life.

The landscape of Ladakh is defined by its towering mountains and arid valleys. The region is home to some of the highest peaks in the world, including K2, the second-highest mountain in the world. The vast expanse of the Ladakh plateau is dotted with shimmering blue lakes, icy glaciers, and vibrant green valleys. The terrain is harsh and unforgiving, but it is also strikingly beautiful.

The people of Ladakh have adapted to this landscape in remarkable ways. They have developed a unique agricultural system that is based on the principles of sustainability and self-sufficiency. The fields are irrigated by the meltwater from the surrounding glaciers, and the crops are grown using traditional farming techniques. The Ladakhis have also developed a rich tradition of handicrafts, including pottery, weaving, and wood carving.

The cultural heritage of Ladakh is equally fascinating. The region has been influenced by its neighbors, including Tibet, India, and Pakistan, but it has retained its distinct identity. The Ladakhis are predominantly Buddhist, and their way of life is deeply intertwined with their religious beliefs. The region is home to numerous monasteries and gompas, which are not only places of worship but also centers of learning and culture.

The Ladakhis are renowned for their hospitality, and their warm and welcoming nature is evident in every aspect of their culture. The region is known for its vibrant festivals, which are celebrated with great fervor and enthusiasm. These festivals provide an opportunity for the Ladakhis to come together, to celebrate their traditions, and to welcome visitors.

One of the most unique aspects of Ladakh is its cuisine. The region is known for its hearty and flavorful food, which is a reflection of the Ladakhis' way of life. The cuisine is based on locally sourced ingredients, including barley, wheat, and vegetables. Meat is also a prominent feature of Ladakhi cuisine, and the local people have developed unique meat dishes, including yak meat and mutton.

As I traveled through Ladakh, I was struck by the simplicity and authenticity of its cuisine. The flavors were robust and earthy, and the dishes were hearty and filling. I sampled dishes like thukpa, a hearty soup made with noodles and vegetables, and momos, a steamed dumpling filled with meat or vegetables. I also tried yak cheese, a local delicacy that is rich and creamy, and chang, a fermented barley drink that is a staple of Ladakhi cuisine.

The mountains of Ladakh are a testament to the resilience of the human spirit. The Ladakhis have managed to carve.

As we descend down the valley, the landscape gradually transforms from stark and rugged mountains to lush green meadows and barley fields. This is where the Indus River flows, the lifeline of Ladakh, providing water for irrigation and drinking. The river is a source of joy and livelihood for the Ladakhi people who depend on it for sustenance.

The cultural experience of Ladakh is just as unique as its landscape. The people of Ladakh have a rich and vibrant culture that is influenced by Buddhism and the harsh environment they live in. They have carved out a living in these rugged mountains, creating a community that is resilient and tightly knit.

As we visit the small towns and villages of Ladakh, we are welcomed with warmth and hospitality. The people here are known for their honesty, integrity, and generosity. They take pride in their culture and are happy to share it with visitors.

We visit the ancient monasteries of Ladakh, including the famous Thiksey and Hemis monasteries. These monasteries are not only spiritual centers but also architectural wonders, built on steep cliffs and adorned with intricate paintings and sculptures.

We also explore the traditional Ladakhi way of life, which revolves around farming, animal husbandry, and handicrafts. The locals are experts in weaving, pottery, and metalwork, and we witness their skills firsthand. We also indulge in traditional Ladakhi cuisine, which is influenced by the harsh climate and the Buddhist way of life.

Our journey to the mountains of Ladakh is not just a physical one but also a spiritual one. The beauty of the landscape, the richness of the culture, and the warmth of the people leave a lasting impression on us, and we return home with a new perspective on life.

CHAPTER EIGHT

"THE ART OF PAPIER MACHE": A LOOK AT THE INTRICATE AND BEAUTIFUL PAPIER MACHE CRAFTS THAT ARE A HALLMARK OF KASHMIRI ART, AND THE DEDICATED ARTISANS

Papier mache is an art form that has been an integral part of the rich culture and tradition of Kashmir for centuries. It involves the use of paper pulp, glue, an

PAPER MACHE

d colors to create intricate, ornate pieces of art that are both beautiful and functional.

The process of creating papier mache involves several steps, each of which requires precision and skill. First, the artisans carve a wooden base that serves as the foundation for the final piece. This is done by skilled craftsmen who carefully carve the wooden base into the desired shape and size.

Next, the paper pulp is prepared by soaking old newspapers or other discarded paper products in water until they turn into a mushy paste. This paste is then mixed with adhesive and applied to the wooden base, forming a smooth and even layer. The artisans then let the piece dry before sanding it down to create a smooth surface.

Once the base layer is complete, the artisans use a variety of tools and techniques to create intricate designs on the surface of the piece. This can include painting, carving, and adding details such as beads or other decorative elements. The process can take days or even weeks, depending on the complexity of the design.

One of the most impressive aspects of papier mache art is the level of detail that can be achieved. The artisans use a variety of tools and techniques to create intricate patterns and designs that are both beautiful and functional. The finished pieces are often used as decorative items, such as vases, bowls, and figurines.

The artisans who create papier mache art are often members of families that have been practicing the craft for generations. They take great pride in their work and are dedicated to preserving this traditional art form for future generations.

In recent years, there has been a renewed interest in papier mache art, both in Kashmir and around the world. Many designers and artists have incorporated papier mache elements into their work, creating a fusion of traditional and contemporary styles.

Overall, the art of papier mache is a testament to the rich cultural heritage of Kashmir and the skill and dedication of its artisans. By continuing to create beautiful and intricate pieces of art, they ensure that this tradition lives on for generations to come.Papier mache is a delicate craft that requires a high level of skill and patience. Each piece is carefully crafted by hand, with multiple layers of paper and glue applied to a mold, which is then meticulously carved and painted with exquisite designs. The artisans who specialize in papier mache have often learned the craft from their families, and they take great pride in their work. Their artistry can be seen in a wide range of products, from small trinket boxes and decorative items to larger pieces of furniture and even entire ceilings. The papier mache tradition has been a part of Kashmiri culture for centuries and continues to thrive today, thanks to the dedication and passion of these skilled artisans.

CHAPTER NINE

"THE GHOSTS OF GULMARG": A HAUNTING TALE OF THE EERIE ABANDONED HOTELS AND SKI RESORTS THAT STAND AS A REMINDER OF THE TROUBLED PAST .

Gulmarg, a town nestled in the Pir Panjal range of the western Himalayas, is one of the most picturesque and popular tourist destinations in the region. Th

GULMARG

e town's reputation as a winter sports destination draws a large number of tourists from all over the world. However, the town has a dark side that is often hidden from view. The abandoned hotels and ski resorts that dot the landscape are a stark reminder of the town's troubled past, and the ghosts that haunt them are a source of fear and fascination for locals and tourists alike.

The story of the abandoned hotels and ski resorts in Gulmarg begins in the late 1980s, during the height of the Kashmir conflict. The town was a hotbed of militant activity, and the Indian army was engaged in a fierce battle with the militants. The hotels and ski resorts were used as safe havens by the militants, who would take refuge in them after carrying out attacks on the army. As a result, the army was forced to evacuate the town, leaving the hotels and ski resorts to be taken over by the militants.

For years, the hotels and ski resorts remained under militant control, serving as training grounds and hideouts for the militants. However, with the decline of militant activity in the region, the hotels and ski resorts were abandoned and left to fall into ruin. Today, the abandoned buildings stand as a reminder of the town's troubled past and the ghosts that haunt them are a source of fear and fascination for locals and tourists alike.

The abandoned hotels and ski resorts in Gulmarg are not just dilapidated buildings; they are also said to be home to ghosts and spirits. Locals and tourists have reported seeing apparitions and hearing strange noises coming from the abandoned buildings. Some have even claimed to have been attacked by the ghosts that haunt the buildings.

One of the most haunted buildings in Gulmarg is the abandoned hotel on the top of the hill. The hotel was once the most luxurious in the town, but now it is a shadow of its former self. The roof has caved in, the walls are crumbling, and the rooms are filled with debris. Locals claim that the hotel is haunted by the ghost of a woman who committed suicide there. They say that her spirit still roams the halls, and that she can be heard weeping at night.

Another haunted building in Gulmarg is the abandoned ski resort at the base of the hill. The resort was once a popular destination for skiers, but now it is an eerie and desolate place. Locals claim that the resort is haunted by the ghosts of the militants who used to use it as a safe haven. They say that the ghosts can be heard whispering and laughing in the corridors, and that their presence can be felt in every room.

Despite the ghosts and the eerie atmosphere that surrounds them, the abandoned hotels and ski resorts in Gulmarg are a popular destination for thrill-seekers and ghost hunters. Tourists flock to the town to experience the thrill of exploring the abandoned buildings and encountering the ghosts that haunt them.

In conclusion, the abandoned hotels and ski resorts in Gulmarg are a haunting reminder of the town's troubled past. The ghosts that haunt them are a source of fear and fascination for locals and tourists alike. While the abandoned buildings may be eerie and desolate, they are also a testament to the resilience of the people of Kashmir, who have endured decades of conflict and unrest. Despite the ghosts and the memories that haunt the town, Gulmarg remains a popular tourist destination, drawing visitors from all over the world to experience its natural beauty and rich culture.

Despite its troubled past, Gulmarg continues to attract tourists with its breathtaking natural beauty and world-renowned ski slopes. Many visitors to the area are fascinated by the ghostly abandoned buildings that remain from the town's past as a playground for the rich and famous.

Walking through the ruins of these abandoned hotels and ski resorts, visitors can't help but feel a sense of unease. The empty halls and crumbling walls are a stark reminder of the region's violent history, and the ghosts that are said to haunt these places only add to the eerie atmosphere.

Some visitors have reported seeing ghostly apparitions in the abandoned hotels and ski resorts, while others have experienced strange noises and sensations. Despite the tales of hauntings, many tourists are still drawn to these abandoned buildings, eager to explore their history and soak up the atmosphere of a bygone era.

Perhaps the most famous of these abandoned buildings is the Grand Palace Hotel, which was once the jewel in Gulmarg's crown. Today, the hotel stands as a ghostly reminder of the violence that tore the region apart, its empty rooms and deserted hallways a testament to the human cost of war and conflict.

While the ghosts of Gulmarg may continue to haunt the abandoned buildings that dot the landscape, the town itself has moved on. Today, it is a bustling hub of activity, with tourists from all over the world coming to enjoy its natural beauty and world-class ski slopes. But for those who take the time to explore its haunted past, Gulmarg remains a place of mystery and intrigue, a place where the past and present are intertwined in fascinating and sometimes terrifying ways.

CHAPTER TEN

“The Road to Amarnath”: A Pilgrimage to the Holy Amarnath Cave, where Thousands of Devotees Brave Treacherous Terrain and Harsh Weather to Pay Homage

The Road to Amarnath: A Journey to the Sacred Cave

AMARNATH CAVE

For centuries, the Amarnath cave has been one of the most sacred sites for Hindu devotees. Located high in the mountains of the Indian state of Jammu and Kashmir, the cave is said to be the abode of Lord Shiva, the Hindu god of destruction and regeneration. Each year, thousands of pilgrims make the arduous journey to the cave, braving treacherous terrain, harsh weather, and other dangers to pay their respects to the deity.

The journey to the Amarnath cave begins in the town of Pahalgam, located about 100 kilometers east of Srinagar, the capital of Jammu and Kashmir. From here, pilgrims must travel by foot or horseback through some of the most rugged and inhospitable terrains on earth. The route winds through steep mountain passes, icy streams, and rocky outcroppings, requiring a level of fitness and determination that many find daunting.

Despite the challenges, however, the pilgrimage remains a deeply spiritual and transformative experience for many who make the journey. Along the way, pilgrims encounter a diverse array of people from all walks of life, united in their shared devotion to Lord Shiva. They also encounter a variety of natural wonders, from the soaring peaks of the Himalayas to the stunning beauty of the Lidder Valley.

One of the most iconic landmarks along the route is the Sheshnag Lake, named after the mythical serpent that is said to dwell in its depths. Pilgrims often stop here to rest and take in the breathtaking beauty of the lake and surrounding mountains.

As the journey continues, the terrain becomes more challenging and the weather more unpredictable. The final stretch of the pilgrimage takes pilgrims through the rugged, windswept terrain of the Amarnath Valley, where the cave is located. Here, they must brave sub-zero temperatures and icy winds to reach their destination.

Despite the hardships, the sight of the Amarnath cave is a powerful and awe-inspiring moment for many pilgrims. The cave itself is small and unremarkable, but the sense of devotion and reverence that permeates the air is palpable. Many pilgrims spend hours in silent meditation and prayer, communing with the divine in a way that is difficult to describe.

In recent years, the pilgrimage to the Amarnath cave has become the subject of controversy and political tension. In 2019, the Indian government imposed a curfew in the region amid fears of violence and terrorism. The move sparked widespread protests and criticism from human rights groups, who argued that it was a violation of the religious freedom of the pilgrims.

Despite these challenges, however, the pilgrimage to the Amarnath cave remains a cherished and deeply meaningful experience for many Hindus. For those who undertake the journey, it is a testament to the enduring power of faith and a reminder of the beauty and majesty of the natural world.

As the trek to the Amarnath cave is long and arduous, pilgrims are advised to undergo medical checkups and be adequately prepared for the journey. The cave is located at an altitude of around 13,500 feet and the trek can take up to five days, depending on the route chosen.

Despite the challenges, thousands of pilgrims make the journey every year, with many citing a sense of spiritual fulfillment and divine intervention as reasons for their visit. It is said that Lord Shiva himself reveals himself to the most devoted of his followers during the pilgrimage.

The route to the Amarnath cave is also known for its breathtaking natural beauty. As pilgrims make their way through steep mountain passes and treacherous paths, they are rewarded with stunning vistas of snow-capped peaks, verdant valleys, and glistening streams. The journey is also an opportunity to experience the warm hospitality and rich culture of the local people, who have lived in this remote and rugged region for generations.

However, the journey to the Amarnath cave is not without its dangers. In recent years, the pilgrimage has been marred by accidents, including landslides and militant attacks. The Indian government has taken several measures to ensure the safety and security of pilgrims, including the deployment of security personnel and the construction of better infrastructure.

In conclusion, the pilgrimage to the Amarnath cave is a unique and unforgettable experience for those who undertake it. It offers an opportunity to connect with one's spirituality and witness the stunning natural beauty of the Kashmir region, all while enduring the challenges of the journey with the support of fellow pilgrims and the local community. However, it is important to undertake the journey with caution and adequate preparation to ensure a safe and successful pilgrimage.

CHAPTER ELEVEN

The enduring myths and legends that have shaped the region.

Kashmir is a region that is located in the northernmost part of India and is characterized by its stunning mountainous landscapes, serene lakes, and idyllic valleys. The region is also rich in history and culture and has been shaped by the influence of different civilizations and cultures over the centuries. In this chapter, we will explore the rich history and culture of Kashmir, including the myths and legends that have endured in the region.

Geography and Early History

The region of Kashmir is located in the northernmost part of India and is surrounded by the Himalayan mountain range. It is bounded by Pakistan to the west, China to the northeast, and India to the south. The region is home to the Jhelum River, which is a major tributary of the Indus River.

The earliest recorded history of Kashmir dates back to the 3rd century BCE when the Mauryan Emperor Ashoka conquered the region. However, it was during the rule of the Kushan Empire in the 1st century CE that Kashmir flourished as a center of Buddhist art and culture. The region was also a hub of trade and commerce, with the famous Silk Road passing through it.

Islam and the Mughal Empire

In the 14th century, Islam was introduced to Kashmir by the Sufi saint Mir Sayyid Ali Hamadani. Religion quickly took hold in the region and had a significant impact on its culture and traditions. The Mughal Empire, which ruled over India in the 16th and 17th centuries, also had a profound influence on Kashmir. The Mughal emperor Akbar the Great visited the region in the 16th century and was so taken by its beauty that he made it his summer capital.

The Mughal influence on Kashmir can be seen in its architecture, art, and cuisine. The famous Mughal gardens, such as the Shalimar Bagh and the Nishat Bagh, are a testament to their love for beauty and nature. The region's rich cuisine also features many Mughal-inspired dishes, such as biryani and kebabs.

The Dogra Rule and British Influence

In the 19th century, Kashmir came under the rule of the Dogra dynasty, which was a Hindu ruler. The Dogra rule had a significant impact on the region's culture and traditions, and they were responsible for the development of infrastructure and the modernization of the region.

The British also had a significant influence on Kashmir during their colonial rule of India. The region became a popular destination for British officials and tourists, who were drawn to its stunning landscapes and natural beauty. The British also introduced new technologies and ideas to the region, which had a significant impact on its culture and society.

The region of Kashmir is steeped in myths and legends that have been passed down through generations, shaping the cultural identity of its people. These stories are often rooted in the region's history, religion, and geography, and continue to hold a special place in the hearts and minds of Kashmiris. In this section, we will explore some of the enduring myths and legends that have shaped the region of Kashmir.

The Legend of the Amarnath Cave

The Amarnath Cave is a sacred site for Hindus and is believed to be the place where Lord Shiva revealed the secrets of creation to his consort, Parvati. The legend goes that a shepherd boy, Buta Malik, was given a bag of coal by a holy man, who told him that it would turn into gold when he reached home. When Buta Malik opened the bag, he found that it contained a lingam, which is a representation of Lord Shiva. The cave is now a popular destination for pilgrims, who trek through the mountains to reach it.

The Legend of the Floating Gardens

Kashmir is known for its beautiful gardens, which have been an integral part of the region's culture and tradition for centuries. One of the most popular legends associated with the gardens is the legend of the floating gardens.

According to the legend, the Mughal emperor Jahangir was so enamored by the beauty of the Kashmiri landscape that he ordered the construction of a garden in the middle of Dal Lake. The garden was built on a series of interconnected floating platforms that were anchored to the lake bed. The platforms were made from willow trees, which were covered with earth and planted with flowers and fruit trees.

The garden was a marvel of engineering and horticulture, and it soon became a popular destination for the Mughal emperors and their courtiers. Visitors would arrive by boat and marvel at the floating garden, which seemed to defy gravity.

Over time, the floating gardens became an integral part of the Kashmiri way of life. The people of Kashmir would use the gardens for fishing, farming, and even as a source of drinking water. The gardens also became a symbol of the region's resilience and ingenuity, as they survived centuries of political turmoil and conflict.

The Legend of the Pir Panjal Range

The Pir Panjal Range is a mountain range in the Himalayas that forms the natural boundary between the Indian states of Jammu and Kashmir and Himachal Pradesh. According to legend, the range was once a vast plain, but a group of mischievous demons stole the plain and hid it in the mountains.

The gods, enraged by the demons' actions, sent a powerful thunderstorm to destroy the demons and their ill-gotten gains. The storm raged for seven days and seven nights, causing massive floods that carved out the mountain range as we know it today.

The Pir Panjal Range is now a popular destination for trekkers and adventurers, who come to explore its rugged terrain and stunning vistas. The legend of the range's creation continues to be passed down through generations, reminding the people of Kashmir of the power of nature and the importance of respecting its forces.

The Legend of the Kashmiri Saffron

Kashmir is known for its high-quality saffron, which is prized for its distinctive flavor and aroma. According to legend, saffron was introduced to Kashmir by a holy man who was on a pilgrimage to Mecca. The man was gifted a saffron bulb by a merchant, who told him that it had magical powers.

When the holy man returned to Kashmir, he planted the bulb in a field and watered it with his tears. The plant grew into a beautiful saffron flower, which soon became famous

The Legend of the Wular Lake

The Wular Lake is the largest freshwater lake in India and is located in the region of Kashmir. According to legend, the lake was created by a powerful sorcerer, who cast a spell to make the part of the mountain and allow the water to flow into the valley.

The sorcerer, who was a devout Muslim, had hoped to create a lake that would bring prosperity and abundance to the region. The lake has since become an important source of fish and water for the people of Kashmir and is an integral part of the region's cultural identity.

The Legend of the Chinar Tree

The Chinar Tree is a majestic tree that is native to the Kashmir region. According to legend, the tree was brought to Kashmir by the famous Persian king, Darius the Great, who planted it in the region as a symbol of his victory over the Greeks.

The tree has since become an important symbol of Kashmiri culture and is often used in traditional art and literature. It is also considered to be a symbol of longevity and resilience, as the tree can live for hundreds of years.

The Legend of the Martand Sun Temple

The Martand Sun Temple is a famous temple in the region of Kashmir that was built during the reign of the Karkota dynasty in the 8th century. According to legend, the temple was built on the site of a fierce battle between the gods and the demons and was dedicated to the Sun god, Surya.

The temple was a masterpiece of ancient architecture and was renowned for its intricate carvings and beautiful sculptures. It was destroyed during the 15th century by the Muslim ruler Sikander Butshikan, who was known for his intolerance towards other religions.

The ruins of the temple are now a popular tourist attraction and serve as a reminder of the rich cultural heritage of the Kashmiri people.

Conclusion

The myths and legends of Kashmir are an important part of the region's cultural identity and have been passed down through generations, shaping the beliefs and values of the people. These stories are often rooted in the region's history, religion, and geography, and continue to hold a special place in the hearts and minds of Kashmiris.

From the legend of the Amarnath Cave to the story of the floating gardens, these myths, and legends offer a window into the rich and diverse cultural heritage of the region. They remind us of the power of nature, the importance of religious devotion, and the resilience of the human spirit in the face of adversity.

12) Introduction

Rivers are often considered the lifeline of a region, providing water, transportation, and fertile land for agriculture. The Jhelum River is no exception, serving as a vital source of water for the people of Kashmir and an important mode of transportation for goods and people. Along the banks of the Jhelum, one can find a rich tapestry of culture, history, and tradition, woven into the fabric of the region. This chapter will take you on a journey along the Jhelum River, exploring the many towns and villages that line its banks, and the people who call them home.

The Jhelum River

The Jhelum River originates from the Verinag spring, located in the southern part of the Kashmir Valley. It flows through the cities of Srinagar, Baramulla, and Uri, before finally entering Pakistan and flowing into the

Indus River. The river is approximately 725 kilometers long and has played a significant role in the history and culture of the region.

Srinagar

Srinagar is the largest city in the Kashmir Valley and is situated on the banks of the Jhelum River. The river divides the city into two parts - the old city on the left bank and the new city on the right bank. The old city is characterized by narrow lanes, bustling bazaars, and historic buildings, while the new city is more modern and developed.

The Jhelum River is an integral part of life in Srinagar, with many of the city's iconic landmarks located on its banks. One such landmark is the Hazratbal Shrine, a revered Islamic shrine that is believed to contain the hair of the Prophet Muhammad. The shrine is located on the left bank of the river and is a popular destination for pilgrims and tourists alike.

Another important landmark on the banks of the Jhelum is the Shankaracharya Temple, a Hindu temple dedicated to Lord Shiva. The temple is perched on top of a hill and offers stunning views of the city and the river below.

Baramulla

Baramulla is a town located approximately 50 kilometers north of Srinagar and is situated on the banks of the Jhelum River. The town has a rich history, with archaeological evidence suggesting that it was inhabited as far back as the 6th century BC.

The Jhelum River is an important source of water for the town, with many of its residents depending on it for agriculture and fishing. The town is also famous for its many historic landmarks, including the Baramulla Fort, a 15th-century fort that was once used by Mughal emperors.

Uri

Uri is a small town located near the Line of Control between India and Pakistan and is situated on the banks of the Jhelum River. The town is known for its scenic beauty, with the river flowing through the town and the mountains providing a stunning backdrop.

The Jhelum River is an important source of water for the town, with many of its residents depending on it for agriculture and fishing. The town is also home to the famous Kaman Aman Setu, a footbridge that connects India and Pakistan and is used by locals to visit relatives and friends on the other side.

The People

The people who live along the banks of the Jhelum River are a diverse group, with different cultures, traditions, and beliefs. However, they all share a common bond - their dependence on the river for their livelihoods.

Many of the people living along the banks of the Jhelum are farmers, growing crops such as rice, wheat, and saffron. They depend on the river for irrigation, and the fertile land along its banks provides the perfect conditions for agriculture.

The river is also an important source of fish, with many residents depending on fishing for their livelihood. In addition to fishing and agriculture, the Jhelum River is also an important mode of transportation, with boats and ferries being used to transport people and goods from one place to another. This has led to the development of many towns and villages along the banks of the river, each with its own unique culture and traditions.

Conclusion

The Jhelum River is not just a body of water that runs through the region, but a symbol of the rich history and culture of Kashmir. It has played a significant role in the lives of the people living along its banks, providing water for agriculture and fishing, and serving as an important mode of transportation. The many towns and villages that line its banks are a testament to the enduring spirit of the people who call this region home, and their deep connection to the river that runs through it.

Thank You For Reading!

"Echoes of the Himalayas: Tales from Kashmir"

Thank you for joining me on this journey through the mystical and enchanting land of Kashmir. It has been a pleasure sharing with you the stories that have been passed down from generations, evoking the echoes of the Himalayas.

Kashmir is a land of stunning beauty, a place where nature manifests itself in its most breathtaking form. The snow-capped peaks, the serene valleys, the gurgling streams, and the tranquil lakes have all served as the backdrop for the stories that have been woven into this book.

Through the pages of this book, I hope I have been able to transport you to this land of enchantment, where time seems to stand still, and where the echoes of the past continue to resonate in the present.

I would like to thank all the people who have contributed to this book, especially the storytellers who have shared their tales with me. I would also like to thank my family and friends for their support and encouragement throughout the writing process.

Lastly, I hope that this book has kindled a sense of curiosity and interest in the rich culture and traditions of Kashmir, and that it has left you with a longing to explore this magnificent land yourself.

Thank you for taking the time to read "Echoes of the Himalayas: Tales from Kashmir". May the echoes of these tales continue to resonate within you, long after you have turned the final page.

Thank you for joining me on this journey through the mystical and enchanting land of Kashmir. It has been a pleasure sharing with you the stories that have been passed down from generations, evoking the echoes of the Himalayas.

Kashmir is a land of stunning beauty, a place where nature manifests itself in its most breathtaking form. The snow-capped peaks, the serene valleys, the gurgling streams, and the tranquil lakes have all served as the backdrop for the stories that have been woven into this book.

Through the pages of this book, I hope I have been able to transport you to this land of enchantment, where time seems to stand still, and where the echoes of the past continue to resonate in the present.

I would like to thank all the people who have contributed to this book, especially the storytellers who have shared their tales with me. I would also like to thank my family and friends for their support and encouragement throughout the writing process.

Lastly, I hope that this book has kindled a sense of curiosity and interest in the rich culture and traditions of Kashmir, and that it has left you with a longing to explore this magnificent land yourself.

Thank you for taking the time to read "Echoes of the Himalayas: Tales from Kashmir". May the echoes of these tales continue to resonate within you, long after you have turned the final page.

Printed by Libri Plureos GmbH in Hamburg,
Germany